LOST

IN TRANSLATION

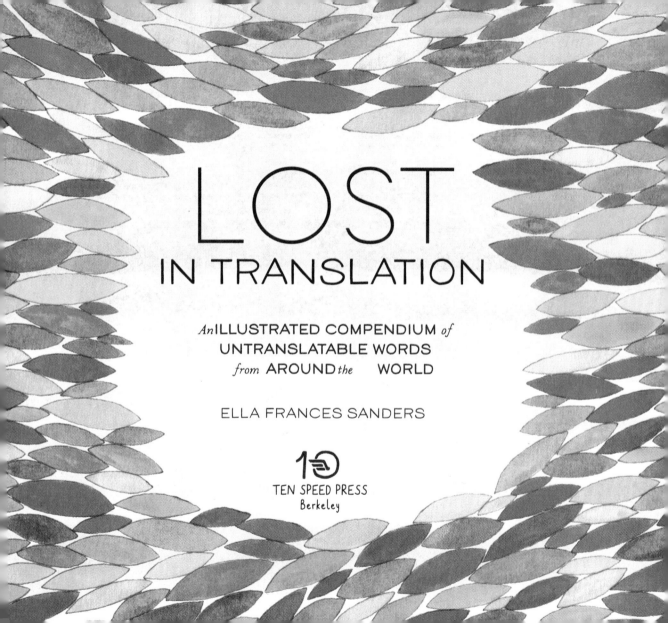

LOST
IN TRANSLATION

An ILLUSTRATED COMPENDIUM *of*
UNTRANSLATABLE WORDS
from AROUND *the* WORLD

ELLA FRANCES SANDERS

TEN SPEED PRESS
Berkeley

INTRODUCTION

How you do introduce the untranslatable?

In our highly connected and communicative world, we have more ways than ever to express ourselves, to tell others how we feel, and to explain the importance or insignificance of our days. The speed and frequency of our exchanges leave just enough room for misunderstandings, though, and now perhaps more than ever before, what we actually mean to say gets lost in translation. The ability to communicate more frequently and faster hasn't eliminated the potential for leaving gaps between meaning and interpretation, and emotions and intentions are misread all too often.

The words in this book may be answers to questions you didn't even know to ask, and perhaps some you did. They might pinpoint emotions and experiences that seemed elusive and indescribable, or they may cause you to remember a person you'd long forgotten. If you take something away from this book other than some brilliant conversation starters, let it be the realization (or affirmation) that you are human, that you are fundamentally, intrinsically bound to every single person on the planet with language and with feelings.

As much as we like to differentiate ourselves, to feel like individuals and rave on about expression and freedom and the experiences that are unique to each one of us, we are all made of the same stuff. We laugh and cry in much the same way, we learn words and then forget them, we meet people from places and cultures different from our own and yet somehow we understand the lives they are living. Language wraps its understanding and punctuation around us all, tempting us to cross boundaries and helping us to comprehend the impossibly difficult questions that life relentlessly throws at us.

Languages aren't unchanging, though they can sometimes hold a false sense of permanence. They do evolve and occasionally die, and whether you speak a few words of one or a thousand words of many, they help to shape us—they give us the ability to voice an opinion, to express love or frustration, to change someone's mind.

For me, making this book has been more than a creative process. It's caused me to look at human nature in an entirely new way, and I find myself recognizing these nouns, adjectives, and verbs in the people I walk by on the street. I see *boketto* in the eyes of an old man sitting at the ocean's edge, and the *resfeber* that has taken over the hearts of friends as they prepare to journey across the world to an unknown culture.

I hope this book helps you find a few long-lost parts of yourself, that it brings to mind fond memories, or that it helps put into words thoughts and feelings that you could never clearly express before. Perhaps you'll find the word that perfectly describes your second cousin once removed, the way you felt two summers ago that you were never able to fully describe, or the look in the eyes of the person sitting across from you right now.

Eckhart Tolle wrote, "Words reduce reality to something the human mind can grasp, which isn't very much." I'm hesitant to agree. Words allow us to grasp and hold onto an extraordinary amount. Sure, all languages can be picked apart and reduced to just a few vowels or symbols or sounds, but the ability that language gives us is incredibly complex. There may be some small essential gaps in your mother tongue, but never fear: you can look to other languages to define what you're feeling, and these pages are your starting point.

So go and get lost in translation.

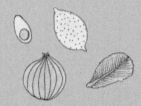

It seems that Norwegians are vague but generous when it comes to sandwiches, as this word can cover most anything that you might consider putting on (or in between) slices of the versatile carbohydrate that is bread. Cheese, meat, peanut butter, lettuce leaves . . . you name it, and it is probably pålegg.

NORWEGIAN

noun

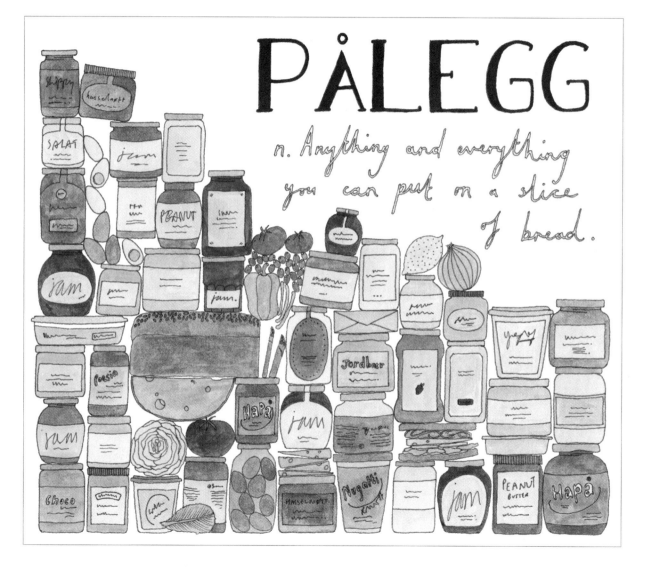

PÅLEGG

n. Anything and everything you can put on a slice of bread.

Maybe you had a single tear rolling down your cheek, or maybe you were crying for days afterward. Touching and powerful stories hit you in the most inexplicable, unexpected, and undeniably human ways.

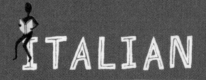

ITALIAN

verb

COMMUOVERE

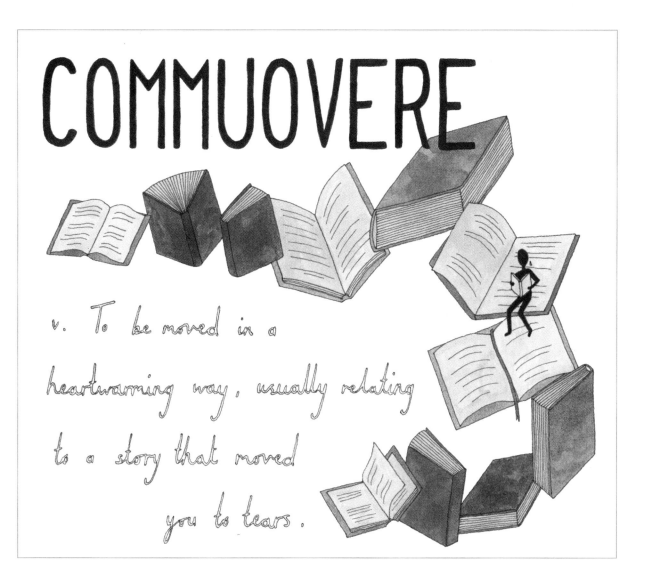

v. To be moved in a heartwarming way, usually relating to a story that moved you to tears.

Perhaps people don't notice these glimmering, lyrical
moments enough anymore, but the way the moon
reflects and leaps across the black water of the
ocean at night is surely a sight to behold.

SWEDISH

noun

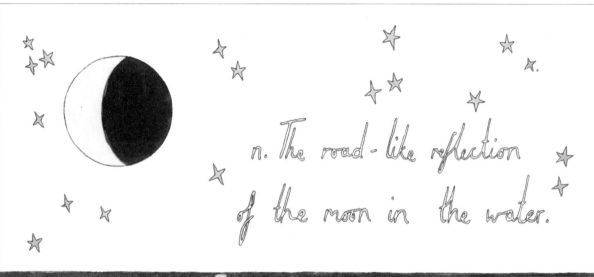

n. The road-like reflection of the moon in the water.

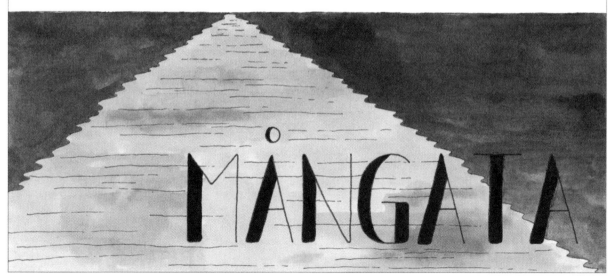

MÅNGATA

When you don't notice the evening bleeding into the night, nor remember the fire changing from hot flames to barely there embers. When you talk for hours about nothing in particular, figure out the meaning of life, and likely drink too much to remember what it was the next morning.

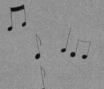

ARABIC

noun

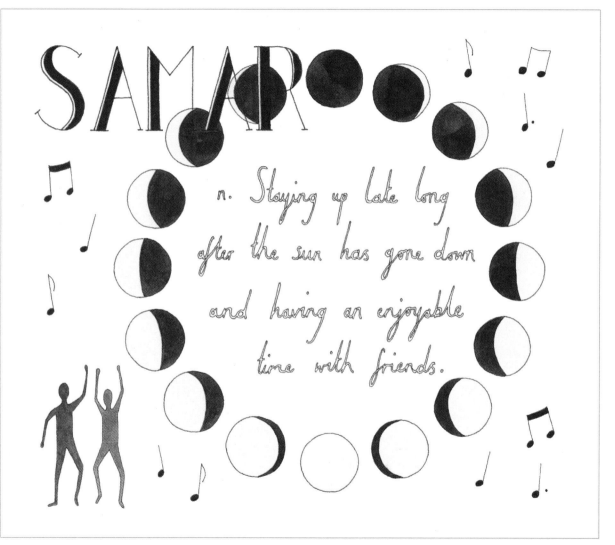

SAMAROO

n. Staying up late long after the sun has gone down and having an enjoyable time with friends.

Ask any Dutch person and they will tell you about *gezellig*. It is something that embodies their warm, welcoming culture, and encompasses all of those things that make you cozy on the inside, like family, good conversations, and hugs.

DUTCH

adjective

GEZELLIG

adj. Describes much more than just coziness – a positive warm emotion or feeling rather than just something physical – and connotes time spent with loved ones, togetherness.

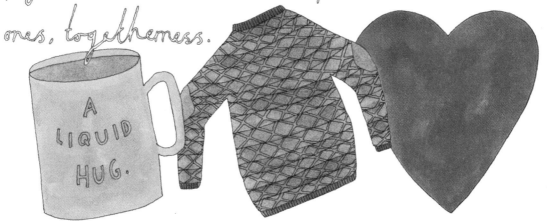

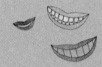

Those sarcastic smiles are not so easy to escape. They make you squirm a little and leave you wishing that you could just slip away without having to return an awkward half-smile.

WELSH

noun

GLAS WEN

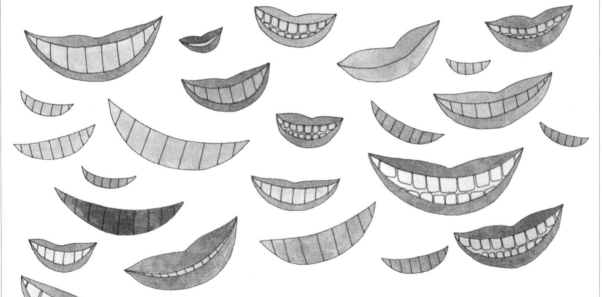

n. This literally means a "blue smile"; one that is sarcastic or mocking.

When you're giving your all, the end result is usually a great one. The concept of *meraki* has obviously grown up around the Greek culture, which seems to emphasize a thoughtful kind of passion and an appreciation for the small things.

GREEK

---

adjective

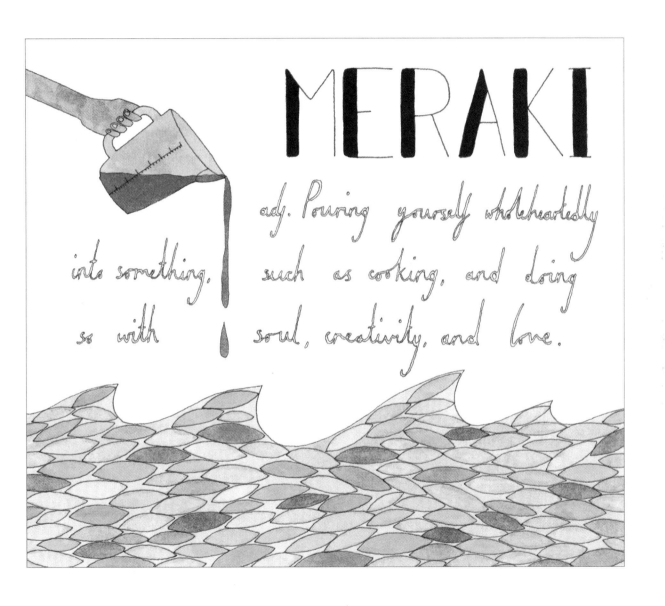

MERAKI

adj. Pouring yourself wholeheartedly into something, such as cooking, and doing so with soul, creativity, and love.

You know exactly what this is. Once it's taken hold, there's no stopping that can't-think-straight, smiling-for-no-reason, spine-tingling feeling that starts somewhere deep inside the walls of your stomach.

TAGALOG

noun

n. The feeling of butterflies in your stomach, usually when something romantic or cute takes place.

KILIG

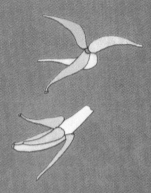

This surely varies from person to person, and from banana to banana, but general consensus is that it takes around two minutes to consume one. In Malay folklore, man-eating ghosts are said to reside in banana trees (*pokok pisang*) during the day.

MALAY

noun

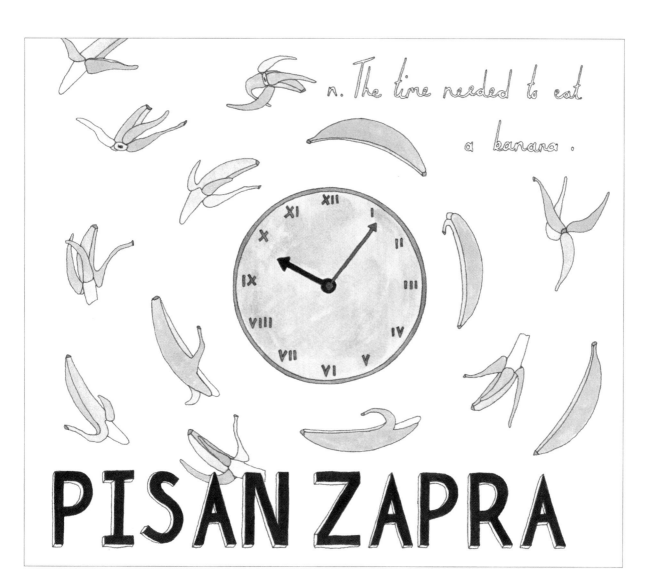

Jugaad has all but become a movement. Solving everyday problems with a combination of frugal innovation and local intelligence, perhaps even bending the rules slightly, brings people's creativity and improvisational skills to the surface.

HINDI

noun

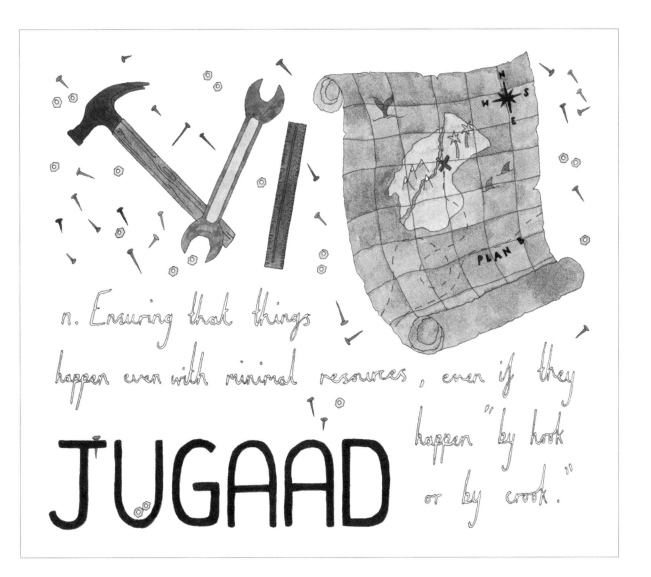

n. Ensuring that things happen even with minimal resources, even if they happen "by hook or by crook."

JUGAAD

The combination of coffee and conversation is a great one, and often leads to inspired exchanges, bright ideas, and general caffeine-induced brilliance. It is perhaps unsurprising that *fika* is a social institution—Swedes have nearly twice the average per capita coffee consumption of the European Union.

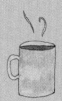

SWEDISH

verb

v. Gathering together to talk and take a break from everyday routines, usually drinking coffee and eating pastries — either at a café or at home — often for hours on end.

FIKA

Hiraeth shares some similarities with the wistfulness of *saudade*, but is a kind of homesickness that the Welsh feel for the Wales of the past, and is tinged with a healthy dose of sadness and longing.

WELSH

noun

n. A homesickness for somewhere you cannot return to, the nostalgia and the grief for the lost places of your past, places that never were.

HIRAETH

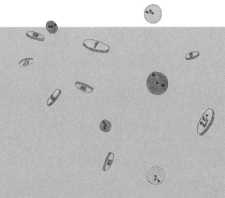

It can be difficult to part with things of value, such as time and money, as they aren't infinite and they can slip through our fingers with surprising ease. We can't get them back once we've given them away, and so wanting to keep them for as long as possible is understandable.

ICELANDIC

verb

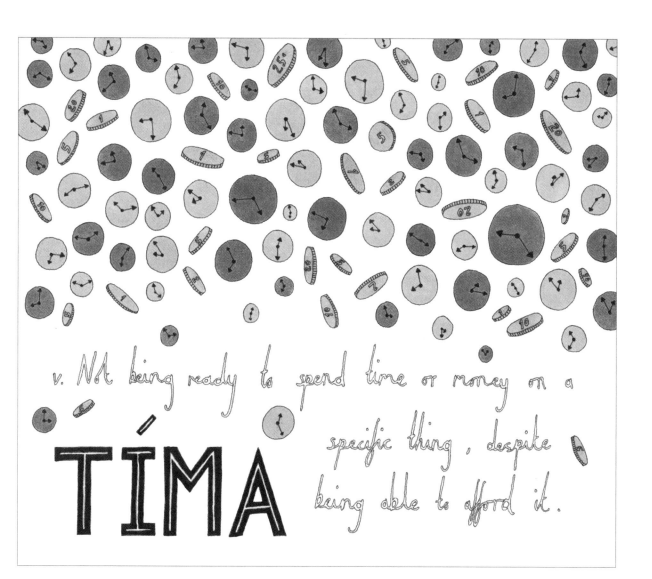

v. Not being ready to spend time or money on a specific thing, despite being able to afford it.

TÍMA

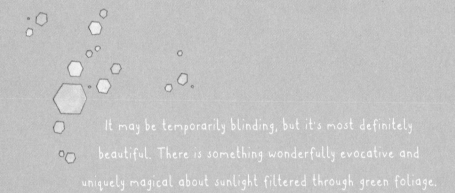

It may be temporarily blinding, but it's most definitely beautiful. There is something wonderfully evocative and uniquely magical about sunlight filtered through green foliage.

JAPANESE

noun

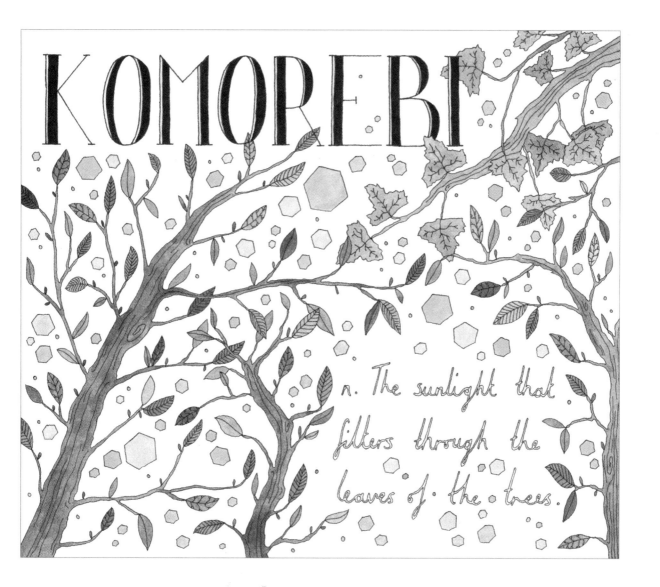

KOMOREBI

n. The sunlight that filters through the leaves of the trees.

Looking at your once-beloved is different somehow—they no longer seem as if sent from the heavens, and there is nothing you can do to stop those wonderful feelings from fading.

RUSSIAN

verb

v. To fall out of love, a bittersweet feeling.

RAZLIUBIT

Sometimes you just have to eat those feelings, and in large quantities. Unfortunately, we are programmed to find comfort in the edible, and until you catch sight of yourself in a reflective surface a month later, it often works.

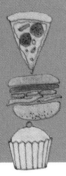

GERMAN

noun

KUMMERSPECK

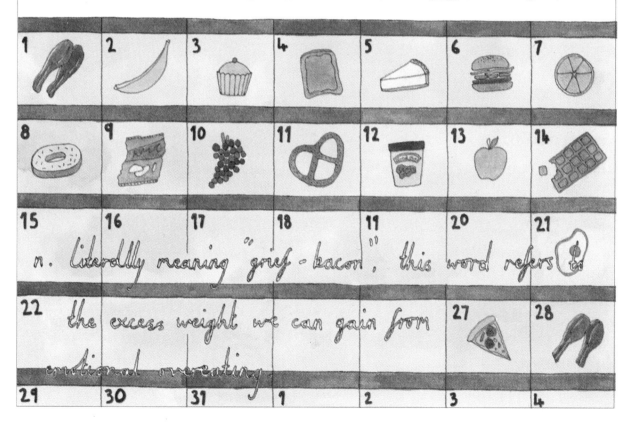

n. literally meaning "grief-bacon", this word refers to the excess weight we can gain from emotional overeating.

It's nice that the Japanese think so highly of thinking about nothing much at all that they actually gave it a name. With the overcrowded and hurried lives we often lead, it can refresh the mind to go wandering, with no destination in particular.

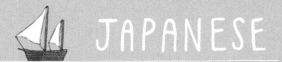

JAPANESE

noun

BOKETTO

n. Gazing vacantly into the distance without really thinking about anything specific.

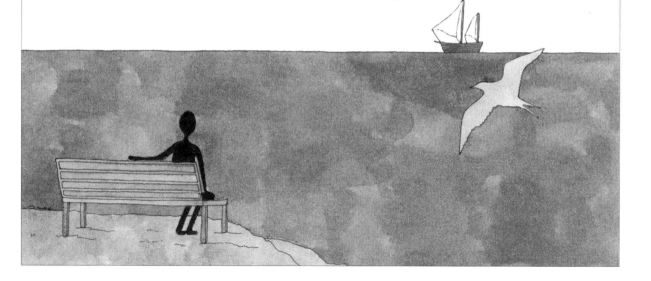

The best laid plans are not usually conducive to spontaneous adventures. Not sure where to go? Great! Throw the map and the plans out the window, and follow your heart for a while instead.

SPANISH

verb

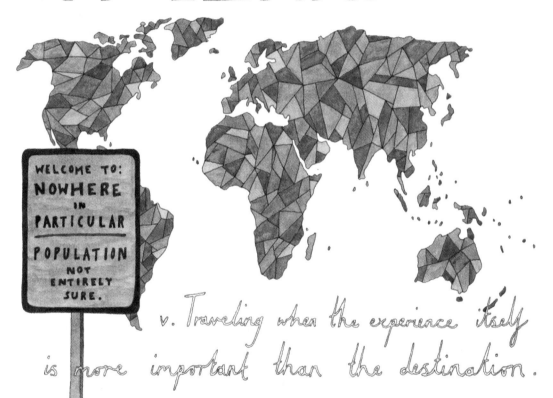

VACILANDO

WELCOME TO:
NOWHERE
IN
PARTICULAR

POPULATION
NOT
ENTIRELY
SURE.

v. Traveling when the experience itself is more important than the destination.

Something we've likely all experienced at one time or another, commonly because our watch was slightly too tight or our socks too small. Tulu, incidentally, is spoken in parts of Southwestern India.

TULU

noun

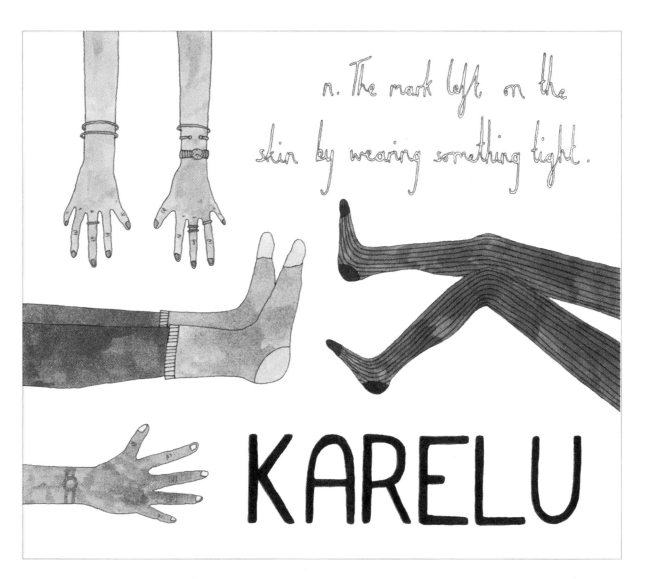

n. The mark left on the skin by wearing something tight.

KARELU

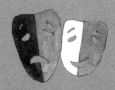

The joke may have been funny for the wrong reasons, but it was funny nonetheless. A complete lack of comic timing? Still hilarious. Forgotten the punch line? Absurdly entertaining.

INDONESIAN

noun

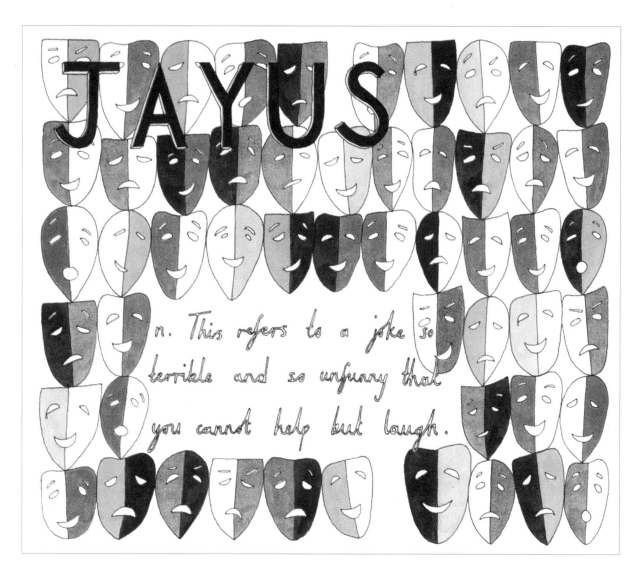

JAYUS

n. This refers to a joke so terrible and so unfunny that you cannot help but laugh.

We all know one. It's not necessarily their fault, but bad things just seem to happen to them . . . all the time. You have two choices when dealing with a *shlimazel*: embrace the chaos that comes with bad luck or run very fast in the other direction.

YIDDISH

noun

SHLIMAZEL

n. Someone who seems to have nothing but bad luck.

This important South African philosophy has various interpretations, but anyone who knows *ubuntu* recognizes that we, as humans, are bound together in ways we cannot see. Another way of putting it, as defined by a Liberian peace activist is, "I am what I am because of who we all are."

NGUNI BANTU

noun

UBUNTU

n. Essentially meaning "I find my worth in you, and you find your worth in me." Can be (very) roughly translated as human kindness.

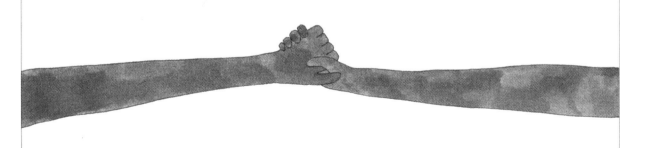

Sure, this sounds like quite a vague measurement, but when you're building a sand castle on the beach and you've decided to create a defensive moat around the king's quarters, this word suddenly makes a lot of sense.

ARABIC

noun

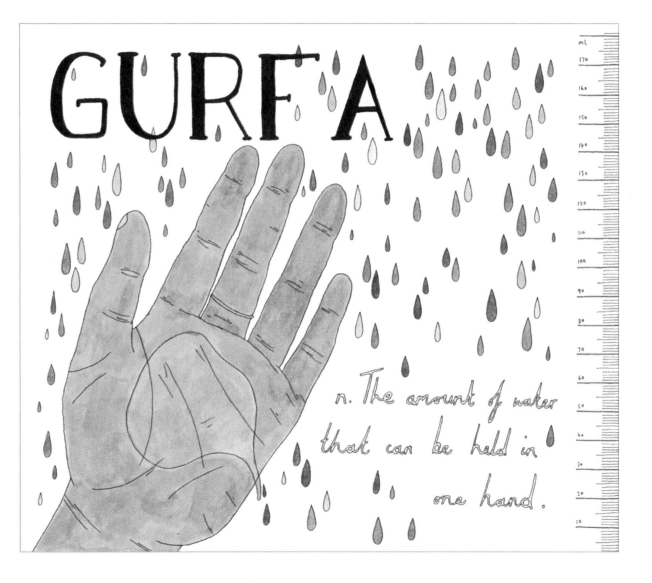

Frustratingly, you always think of the best lines as you're walking away. As usual, that sarcastic and biting—yet hilarious—comeback occurs to you only as you turn the corner, or have reached the bottom of the stairs.

YIDDISH

noun

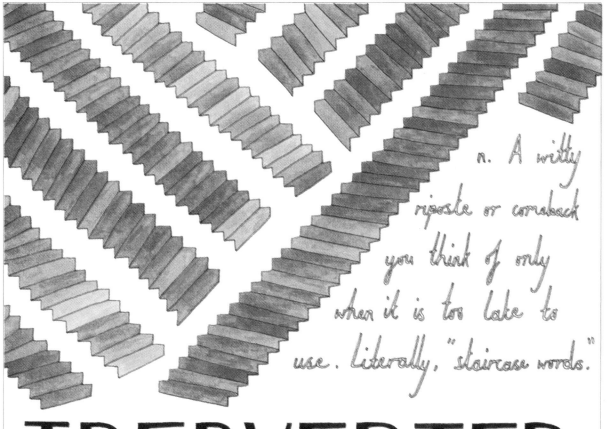

n. A witty riposte or comeback you think of only when it is too late to use. Literally, "staircase words."

TREPVERTER

When trouble arises, bury your head in the sand and pretend that there aren't any problems, and avoid any involvement until things go back to normal. Actually, don't take this approach, as it never ends well. Carrying on without addressing the real issues is a practice so widespread that the Dutch have pinned it down and named it. Which is impressive, seeing as ostriches can run at 31 miles/50 kilometers an hour.

DUTCH

noun

STRUISVOGELPOLITIEK

n. Literally, "ostrich politics." Acting like you don't notice when something bad happens and continuing on regardless, as you normally would.

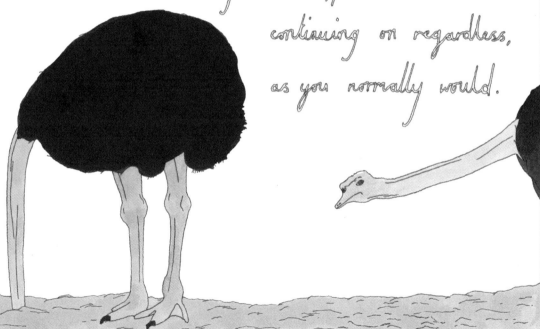

Derived from Buddhist teachings, this is a Japanese
aesthetic centered around discovering beauty in
imperfections and incompleteness. An acceptance of
our transience and the asymmetry within our lives can
lead us to a more fulfilling yet modest existence.

JAPANESE

noun

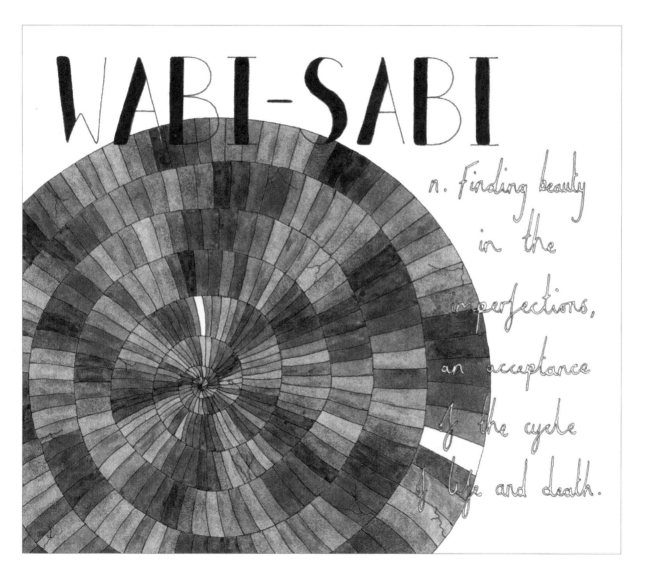

WABI-SABI

n. Finding beauty in the imperfections, an acceptance of the cycle of life and death.

A word so difficult to spell, it aptly reflects the tangled
and incomprehensible nature of this look. Fittingly, Yaghan
is an indigenous language of distant Tierra del Fuego, Chile.

YAGHAN

noun

n. A silent acknowledgement and understanding between two people, who are both wishing or thinking the same thing (and are both unwilling to initiate).

MAMIHLAPINATAPAI

You've been counting down the days, and now you're counting down the hours. Your heart knows that it's going on a journey and you cannot sit still as a result. So pick up your backpack, put on your boots, and go boldly into the adventure and the unexpected!

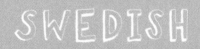

SWEDISH

noun

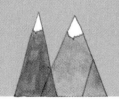

n. The restless beat of a traveler's heart before the journey begins, a mixture of anxiety and anticipation.

RESFEBER

Maybe they are just anybody, or maybe they are clearly somebody special, but there is something resembling a small sliver of sunlight in your eyes, and you are happy to have met them.

FARSI

noun

TIÁM

n. The twinkle in your eye when you first meet someone.

This probably lies somewhere between romantic and morbid, and is perhaps the most beautiful yet disturbing way of letting someone know that you'd quite like them to stick around for a while.

ARABIC

noun

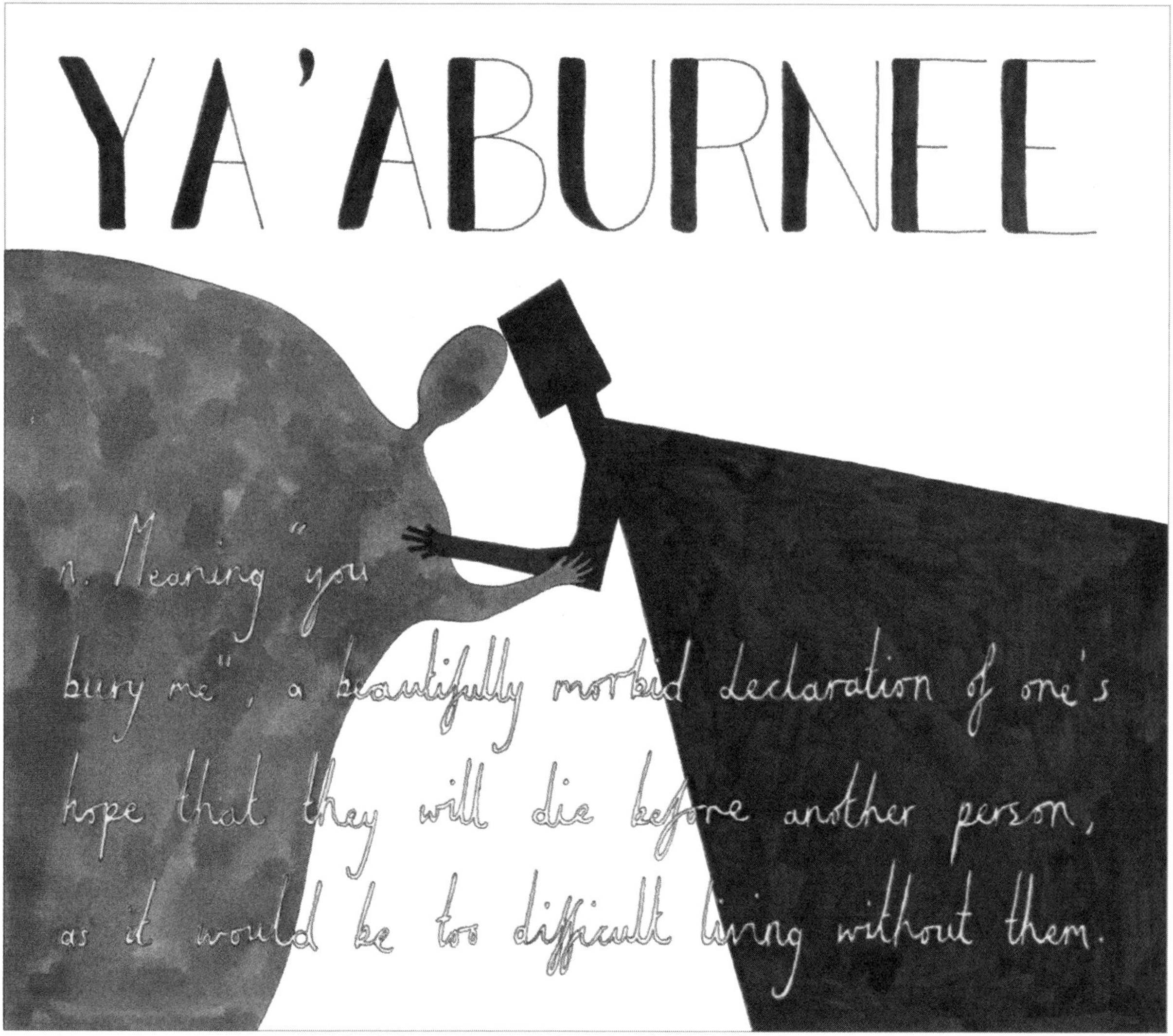
YA'ABURNEE
n. Meaning "you bury me", a beautifully morbid declaration of one's hope that they will die before another person, as it would be too difficult living without them.

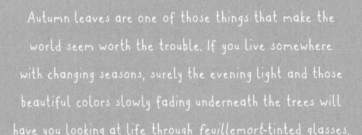

Autumn leaves are one of those things that make the world seem worth the trouble. If you live somewhere with changing seasons, surely the evening light and those beautiful colors slowly fading underneath the trees will have you looking at life through *feuillemort*-tinted glasses.

FRENCH

adjective

FEUILLEMORT

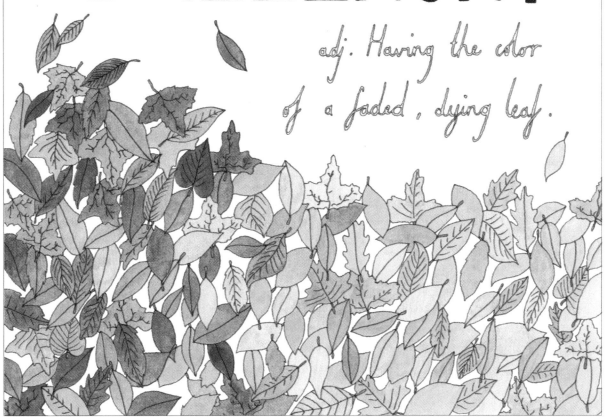

adj. Having the color of a faded, dying leaf.

This may seem like a very imprecise and rather unpredictable way to measure distance, but actually it's pretty widely acknowledged (in reindeer circles at least) that a *poronkusema* is around 4.7 miles/7.5 kilometers.

FINNISH

noun

PORONKUSEMA

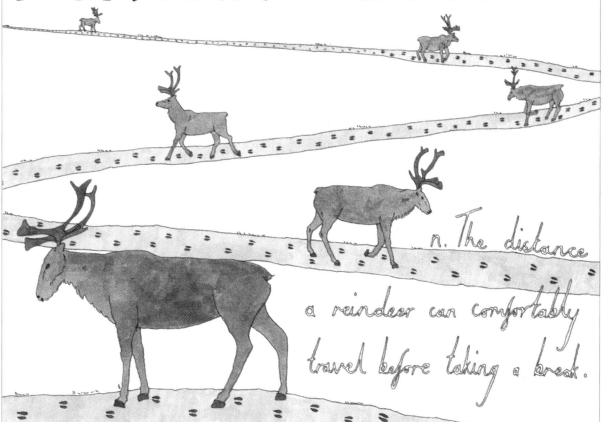

n. The distance a reindeer can comfortably travel before taking a break.

It's too easy to get comfortable, to stop challenging yourself, and then to stop finding it necessary to even leave the house. We are meant to try and fail, to take leaps of faith, only to land facedown on the floor. So go and take an icy cold shower or two.

GERMAN

noun

n. Refers to someone who would only take a warm shower (not an icy cold or burning hot one), implying that they are a bit of a wimp, and unwilling to step outside of their comfort zone.

WARMDUSCHER

Sometimes it can be difficult to know if that look is
one of anxiety or anger, or of tenderness or sadness,
but over time you learn to tell the difference.

KOREAN

noun

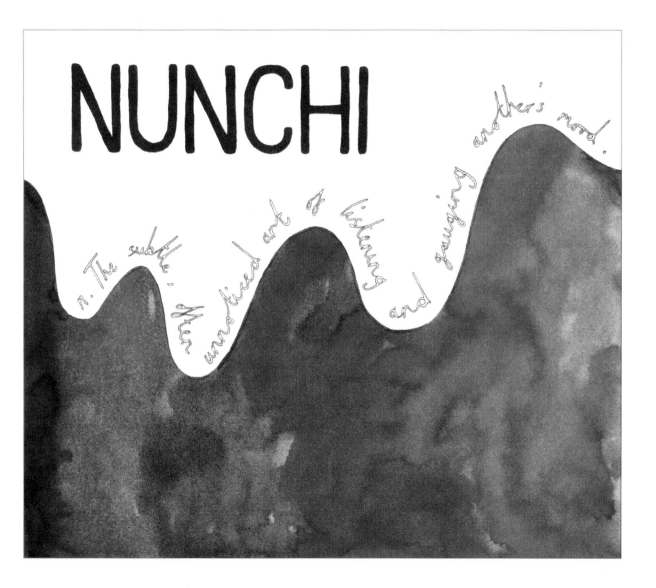

NUNCHI

n. The subtle, often unnoticed art of listening and gauging another's mood.

When they explained how to get there, their directions all made perfect sense—you nodded and looked back with clear understanding. Then you parted ways, and now you can't remember whether to take a left or a right.

HAWAIIAN

noun

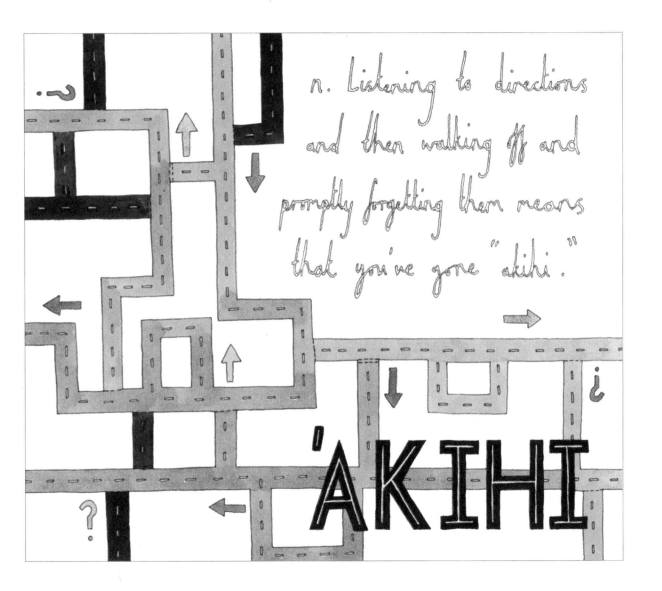

Whether you are searching for something tangible (like a perfectly shaped pebble) or something intangible (like an answer to one of life's many questions), it can probably be found in the wise, all-encompassing oceans. Or sometimes in rivers, lakes, and streams. And on occasion, in puddles. (Wagiman is a nearly-extinct Australian language.)

WAGIMAN

verb

MURR-MA

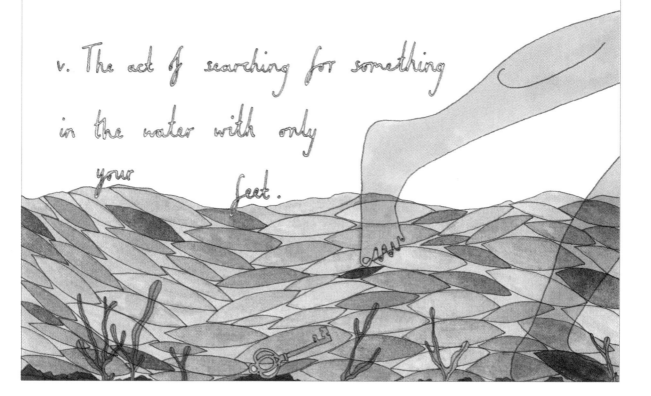

v. The act of searching for something in the water with only your feet.

Goya is the realm of make-believe, of amazing stories that make you forget what you're doing and where you are—stories that give you wings and send you soaring across mountain ranges that you never knew existed or voyaging across oceans even though you don't know how to sail.

URDU

noun

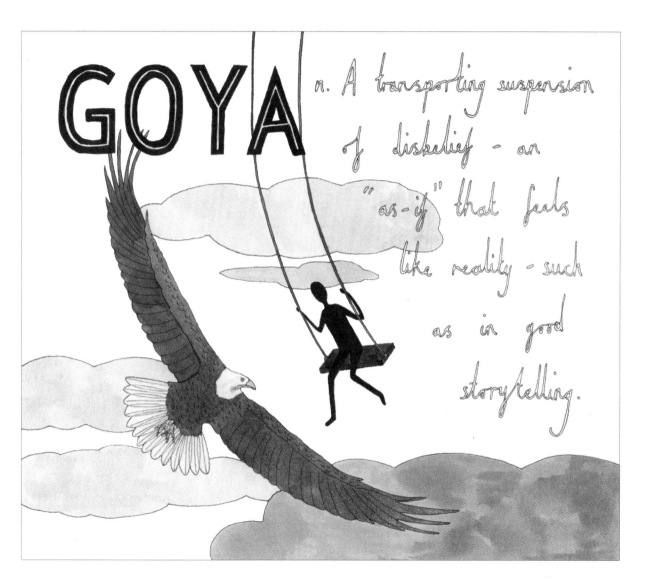

GOYA *n.* A transporting suspension of disbelief — an "as-if" that feels like reality — such as in good storytelling.

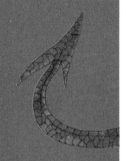

Fire-breathing dragons are not to be taken lightly.
Whether he came home three hours late or he forgot your
anniversary because he was watching basketball, buying
your forgiveness shouldn't really work, but it often does.

GERMAN

noun

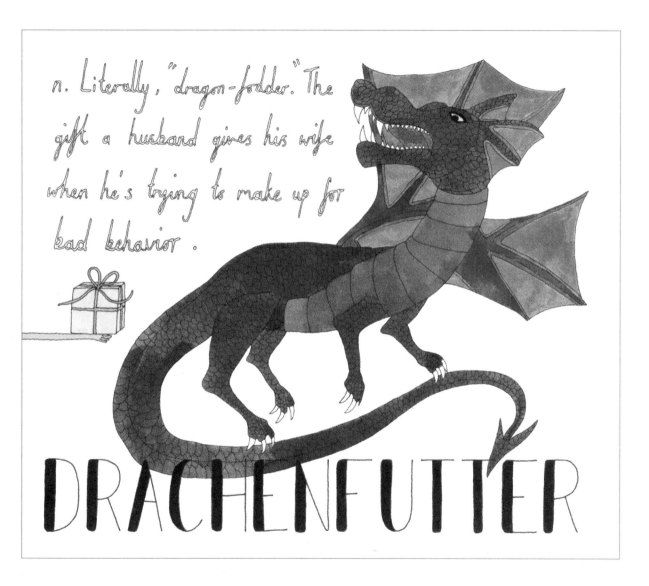

n. Literally, "dragon-fodder." The gift a husband gives his wife when he's trying to make up for bad behavior.

DRACHENFUTTER

Call it intuition, call it good vibes or a gut instinct, sometimes you just know that the person you just met is wonderful. And it's usually best to let them know.

HUNGARIAN

adjective

SZIMPATIKUS

adj. When meeting someone for the first time, and your intuition tells you that they are a good person, you can refer to them as "szimpatikus."

Somewhere between impatience and anticipation is a feeling
that compels you to go outside and inside, and outside and then
inside again, to check if someone is walking over the hill or
around the corner. Does time pass more quickly when doing this?
Possibly.

INUIT

noun

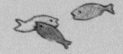

IKTSUARPOK

n. The act of repeatedly going outside to keep checking if someone (anyone) is coming.

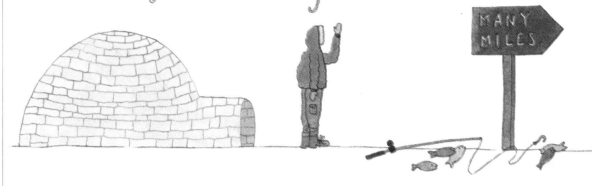

Maybe this is something you've yet to experience, or maybe you've had it happen to you repeatedly. Either way, it's wonderful. Research has shown that *forelsket* is most likely to occur when you wear your heart on your sleeve.

NORWEGIAN

noun

FORELSKET

n. The indescribable euphoria experienced as you begin to fall in love.

Whether you read this and think, "Only three cups?" or you don't understand how it's possible to stomach even one cup of coffee, let alone three, you have to admit that this is a very logical and efficient word.

SWEDISH

noun

n. On its own, "tår" means a cup of coffee and "patår" is the refill of said coffee. A "tretår" is therefore a second refill, or a "threefill."

TRETÅR

The *tsundoku* scale can range from just one unread book
to a serious hoard, so you are most likely guilty of it.
As intellectual as you may look tripping over an unread
copy of *Great Expectations* on your way to the front door,
those pages probably deserve to see the daylight.

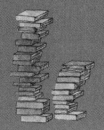

JAPANESE

noun

TSUNDOKU

n. Leaving a book unread after buying it, typically piled up together with other unread books.

It's unavoidable, and usually a sign that things are about to get serious. Alcohol percentage has little to do with it—rather you can almost sense the generations of whiskey drinkers before you, sitting in dark, smoke-filled bars in the dim light before the dawn.

GAELIC

noun

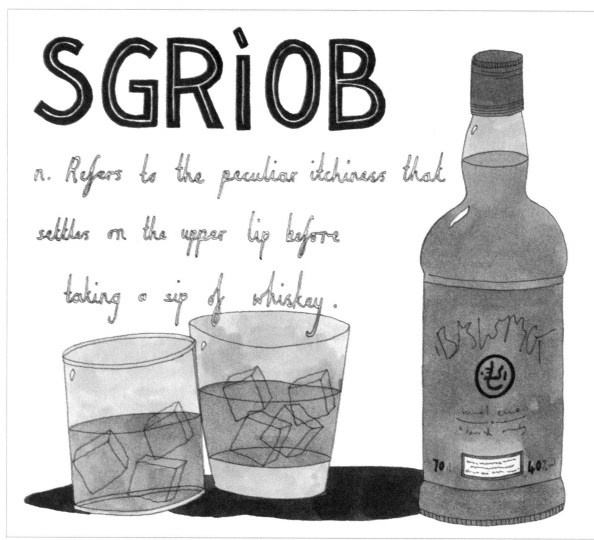

SGRÌOB

n. Refers to the peculiar itchiness that settles on the upper lip before taking a sip of whiskey.

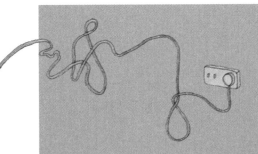

Cables love to tangle. Turn your back on them for one second
and then you will have to spend days putting them back in order,
quickly discovering whether or not you have real patience.

GERMAN

noun

KABEL SALAT

n. A word to describe a
mess of very tangled cables,
literally a "cable-salad."

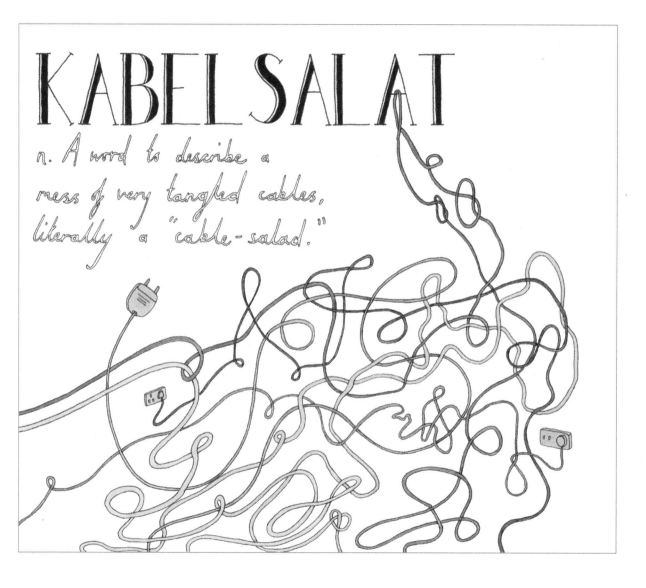

Knowing there are people who would follow you to the ends of the earth and back again puts a certain spring in your step and a certain kind of smile on your face.

URDU

noun

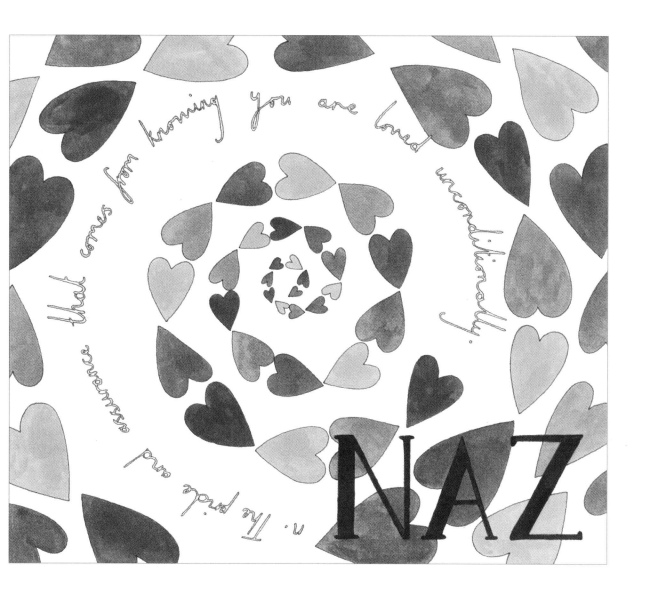

The pride and assurance that comes from knowing you are loved unconditionally.

NAZ

Your head is in the clouds and you aren't coming down anytime soon. You're living in a dream world—the 9-to-5 has no place here and paperwork doesn't exist at this altitude. So it's out with reality and in with the impractical.

YIDDISH

noun

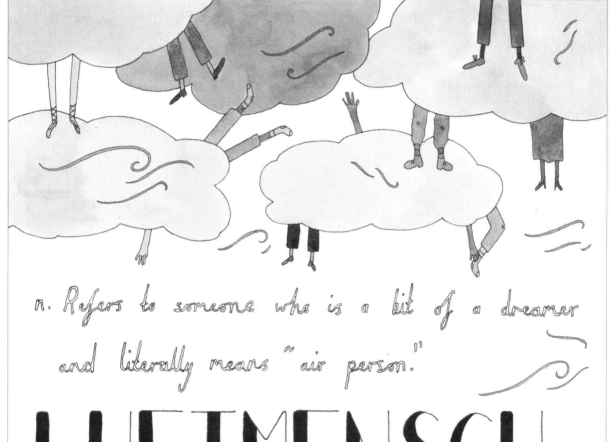

n. Refers to someone who is a bit of a dreamer and literally means "air person."

LUFTMENSCH

A sentiment much stronger than simply missing something or someone, *saudade* has been (and continues to be) the subject of some beautiful, heartbreaking art and literature. It seems to take on nuances from country to country and person to person— Brazil even celebrates a day of *saudade* every January.

PORTUGUESE

noun

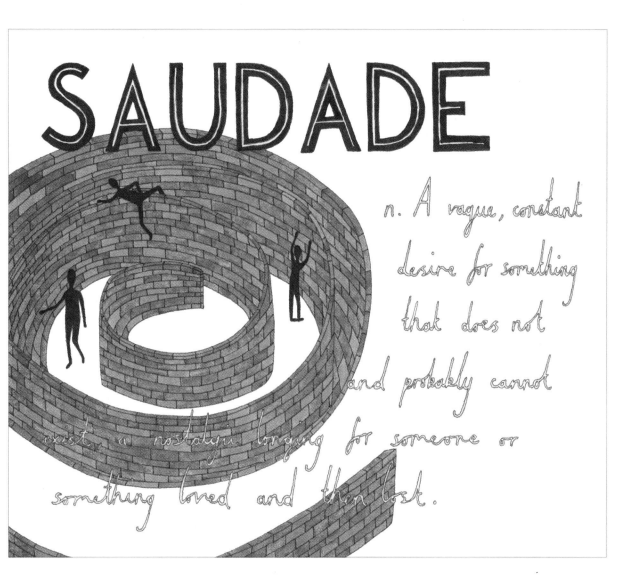

SAUDADE

n. A vague, constant desire for something that does not and probably cannot exist; a nostalgic longing for someone or something loved and then lost.

Perhaps now more of a man-under-40 fashion policy
than schoolboy sloppiness, a *cotisuelto* is usually
a man who wears the right size of shirt and who is at
ease with both the world and his wardrobe choices.

CARIBBEAN SPANISH

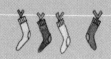

noun

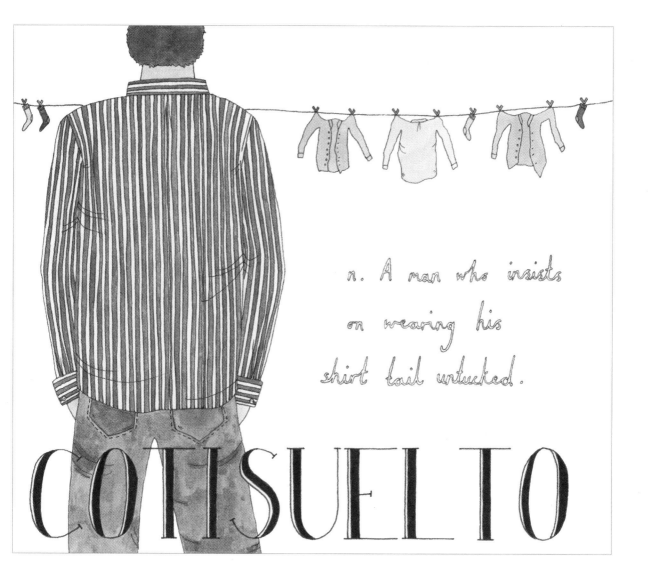

n. A man who insists on wearing his shirt tail untucked.

CONSUELTO

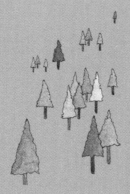

A feeling that most of us don't often experience anymore,
as city parks are a poor substitute for the woods. It seems
that we are connected to just about everything except nature,
where reality can be allowed to slip away between the
branches. Your soul will thank you for some time in the trees.

GERMAN

noun

WALDEINSAMKEIT

n. The feeling of being alone in the woods, an easy solitude and a connectedness to nature.

It's perhaps not surprising that in a country filled with people so perfectly in tune with their emotions and sensuality, there's a word for this quintessential lover's act. We can definitely learn to love people simply for the scent of their shampoo, and there is something reassuring about a trusted hand entwined in your tresses.

BRAZILIAN PORTUGUESE

noun

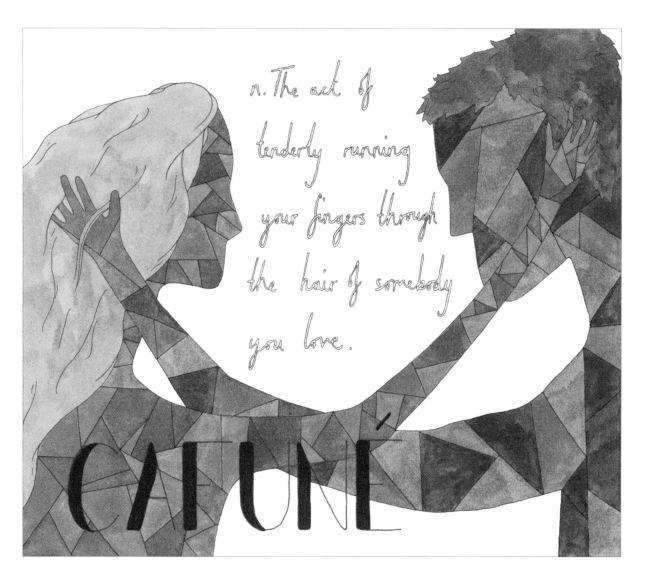

n. The act of tenderly running your fingers through the hair of somebody you love.

CAFUNÉ

We can't feel it, but we might sometimes be able to sense it. The planets are spinning faster than we could ever possibly run and the stars, which never appear to change, aren't going to remain in the sky forever.

SANSKRIT

noun

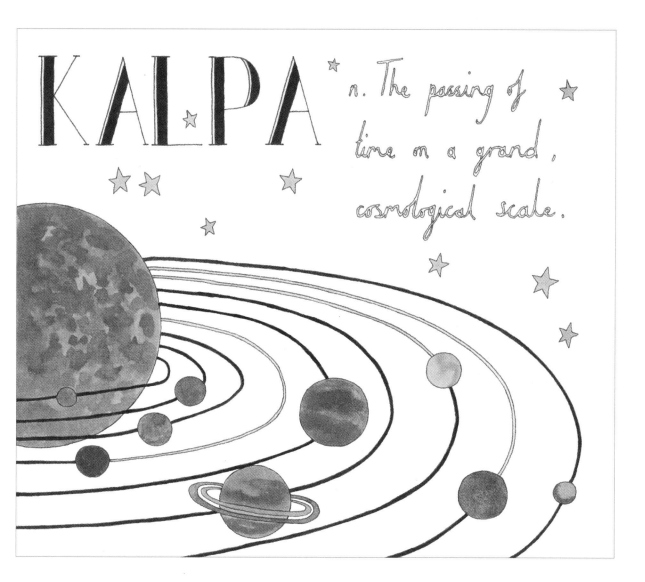

ACKNOWLEDGMENTS

A lot of worlds collided in order to make this book happen, and I'm so glad that they did. These acknowledgments are more like an expression of heartfelt and eternal thanks, mostly for putting up with me.

If I could marry both my agent and my editor, I would. Elizabeth, Kaitlin—from the beginning of this process your words were too kind and your encouragement too encouraging, so thank you. There may be a large expanse of water between us, but the Atlantic Ocean means surprisingly little when we are bound together by a book. Sarah, you made this thing beautiful—thank you. Jonny, thank you for having a good idea. To all the people who I've emailed but never met in person, thank you for being dragged into this. To the rest of the publishing world, thanks for letting me join your club; I hope that we'll be making endpapers together for a long time to come.

To those small miracles currently sitting in my family tree, thank you for keeping this unreliable boat afloat. We all know that I wouldn't be here without you. Yes, Dean, the tree includes you.

And, of course, thank you, because it's always been you and it always will be.